PRAISE for *Nursery Rhymes in Black*

"Latorial Faison embodies the creed, 'She who gives love / Must learn to organize pain,' for her embrace of the joyful and often sorrowful experiences of Black life is accomplished with such cultural precision and old-fashioned wisdom. She demands from us a listen."
—DR. JOANNE VEAL GABBIN, founder of the Furious Flower Poetry Center and executive director of The Wintergreen Women Writers Collective

"These heart-stopping poems transport us through the life-journey of a Southern mother, an orphan who became a widely respected elder. Faison, her mournful daughter, uses deep grieving as the vehicle to move this body of poems. This is a mother who, in spite of strict segregation, was a valiant, seemingly invincible parent, even facing down terminal cancer. In the midst of putting her mother on a pedestal, though, the poet shows the fault-lines of common mortals. The daughter/poet celebrates the mother/near-to-an-angel in glorious phraseology. 'Black & woman / you always rose again . . . a whole cloud of witnesses weeping.' But Mama was also a practical goddess who kept up insurance policies on everybody in the household, what the poet ironically calls 'a way to go fund ourselves.' These poems explain the Black Holy Ghost, the 'white Jesus / Hanging high' on frames in Black living rooms, the lynching tree, post–Jim Crow, Southampton County, VA, and slow integration. But the poems about Mama ground the collection and elevate it simultaneously."
—JUDY JUANITA, author of *Virgin Soul* and *The Black Experience in Four Genres*

"Creatively constructing the intricacies of memory and familial advice associated with small-town Virginia, Latorial Faison probes African American and family history, parent/child relationships, work, sexuality, racial interactions, racism, and death/loss/grief. With strong feminine influences that shaped her life, Faison celebrates that strength, its basis in a sometimes-problematic religion, and its transcendence

of that origin. Mother and grandmother figures are always near, and their loss, as in 'How to Bury Your Mama,' may shake the foundations for a moment, but the tradition from which they come thrives. *Nursery Rhymes in Black* captures a time and a place that are no less powerful because they are more memory than just down the street. Faison invites readers to see that world, that light, those lives, that history through the eyes of a faithfully attentive observer and analyst."
—TRUDIER HARRIS, author of *Summer Snow: Reflections from a Black Daughter of the South* and *Bigger: A Literary Life*

"A masterful love letter to her mother, with each verse serving as both tribute and deep reflection. The beautiful opening poem, 'Mama as a Negro Spiritual,' locates, orients us, and sets the tone for the entire collection. The poet observes her mother's ability to transform pain into love and the effort it requires. Her mother is revealed as Ms. Shirley, the lunch lady; the bus driver; Sammy's wife; and a boundless giver of self. The poet is boundless too and grapples with the realities of Virginia, particularly Southampton County. While acknowledging that past injustices cannot be undone, Faison confronts them head on. *Nursery Rhymes in Black* stands as a testament to the power of bearing witness—to both people and place—as a means of claiming individual and generational space. It's an act of speaking out during hardship and grief, a full-throated Hallelujah Anyhow!"
—GLENIS REDMOND, author of *The Listening Skin* and *The Song of Everything*

"Latorial Faison's debut is above all a meditation upon the heart of a loving Black mother, a Proverbs 31 woman as apt to quote headlines from the latest copy of *The Tidewater News* as she is to quote scripture. Mama prepares for rainy days and dying breaths, keeps a dollar in her pocket, and knows her way around her white folks like she knows her kitchen. She inculcates her children with a faith that has sustained her and surrounds them with ancestors who are proof of abundant life in this rural Virginia county best known for Nat Turner's rebellion. Faison's Courtland is no New Jerusalem—after all, here are segregation academies and old hanging trees—but there is its Ridley Road. Let us sing of Youth Dew, penny candy, and Easter Sunday dinner on this side of Jordan."
—CEDRIC TILLMAN, author of *Lilies in the Valley* and *In My Feelins*

NURSERY RHYMES IN BLACK

ALASKA LITERARY SERIES
PEGGY SHUMAKER, SERIES EDITOR

The Alaska Literary Series publishes poetry, fiction, and literary nonfiction. Successful manuscripts have a strong connection to Alaska or the circumpolar north, are written by people living in the far north, or both. We prefer writing that makes the northern experience available to the world, and we choose manuscripts that offer compelling literary insights into the human condition.

Armor and Ornament by Christopher Lee Miles
Be-Hooved by Mar Ka
Benchmarks by Richard Dauenhauer
Cabin, Clearing, Forest by Zach Falcon
Cabin 135 by Katie Eberhart
The City Beneath the Snow by Marjorie Kowalski Cole
Cold Latitudes by Rosemary McGuire
Cold Spell by Deb Vanasse
The Cormorant Hunter's Wife by Joan Kane
The Creatures at the Absolute Bottom of the Sea by Rosemary McGuire
Ends of the Earth by Kate Partridge
Gaining Daylight by Sara Loewen
The Geography of Water by Mary Emerick
Human Being Songs by Jean Anderson
I Follow in the Dust She Raises by Linda Martin
In the Quiet Season and Other Stories by Martha Amore
Just Between Us by David McElroy
A Ladder of Cranes by Tom Sexton
Leavetakings by Corinna Cook
Li Bai Rides a Celestial Dolphin Home by Tom Sexton
Of Darkness and Light by Wendy Erd
Oil and Water by Mei Mei Evans
Old Woman with Berries in Her Lap by Vivian Faith Prescott
Overwinter by Jeremy Pataky
The Rabbits Could Sing by Amber Flora Thomas
River of Light by John Morgan and Kesler Woodward
Roughly for the North by Carrie Ayagaduk Ojanen
Sailing by Ravens by Holly J. Hughes
Spirit Things by Lara Messersmith-Glavin
Threadbare by Mary Kudenov
Trouble will Save You by David Nikki Crouse
Uncommon Weather by Richard Chiappone
Upriver by Carolyn Kremers
Water Mask by Monica Devine
Water the Rocks Make by David McElroy
Whiteout by Jessica Goodfellow
Wild Rivers Wild Rose by Sarah Birdsall

Nursery Rhymes in Black

Latorial Faison

PERMAFROST PRIZE SERIES

UNIVERSITY OF ALASKA PRESS

Fairbanks

© 2025 by University Press of Colorado

Published by University of Alaska Press
An imprint of University Press of Colorado
1580 North Logan Street, Suite 660
PMB 39883
Denver, Colorado 80203-1942

All rights reserved

 The University Press of Colorado is a proud member of Association of University Presses.

The University Press of Colorado is a cooperative publishing enterprise supported, in part, by Adams State University, Colorado School of Mines, Colorado State University, Fort Lewis College, Metropolitan State University of Denver, University of Alaska Fairbanks, University of Colorado, University of Denver, University of Northern Colorado, University of Wyoming, Utah State University, and Western Colorado University.

ISBN: 978-1-64642-727-7 (paperback)
ISBN: 978-1-64642-734-5 (ebook)
https://doi.org/10.5876/9781646427345

Library of Congress Cataloging-in-Publication Data

Names: Faison, Latorial author
Title: Nursery rhymes in Black / Latorial Faison.
Other titles: Nursery rhymes in Black (Compilation)
Description: Fairbanks : University of Alaska Press, 2025. | Series: Permafrost prize series
Identifiers: LCCN 2025001862 (print) | LCCN 2025001863 (ebook) | ISBN 9781646427277 paperback | ISBN 9781646427345 ebook
Subjects: LCSH: African Americans—Poetry | LCGFT: Poetry
Classification: LCC PS3606.A38 N87 2025 (print) | LCC PS3606.A38 (ebook) | DDC 811.6—dc23/eng/20250411
LC record available at https://lccn.loc.gov/2025001862
LC ebook record available at https://lccn.loc.gov/2025001863

Covert art: © Delita Martin, Night Garden, edition 8 of 10, 2022. Relief printing, decorative paper, hand stitching, colored pencil, 30 x 40 inches. Courtesy of the artist.

To *Mama and Daddy*, the grandparents who raised me, the late Samuel and Shirley Lee Turner Williams, to my husband *Carl Jerome*, to our legacy—our three sons: *Carl, Kendall & Kaleb*, to the historic, episodic memory of our Southampton County, Virginia, life and upbringing, to all of our different, yet amazing parents, grandparents, aunts, uncles, family members, friends, and villages of support, to the countless, significant other people whose lives have intersected with ours, and to all who, in many remarkable, extraordinary ways, have lived to tell the African American story, *how we overcome*.

Contents

FOREWORD *Ariana Benson* ix

Mama Was a Negro Spiritual   5
Witness   7
History Woman   8
I am Not Ashamed of Your Gospel   10
Self-Portrait   12
Mama Sang the Blues   13
Sundays   15
Fast Girls   16
Abominations   17
Young's Literal Translation   18
I Know It Was the Blood   19
Hallelujah Anyhow   20
Our Town   22
I'm So Courtland   24
Forbidden Fruit   26
Important Papers   27
Girl, 1983   29
When We Fall on Our Knees   31
Judas Kiss   33
Black and Forth   34
Testify   38
Where Is God?   39
When a Monarch Dies   40
Heaven   41
This Place   42
The Un-Praised   43

She Who Gives Love 44
Outside the Picture Window 45
A Whole Town's Eyes 46
How to Bury Your Mama 47
The Last Easter 50
Tribulation 51
A Shroud for Mother's Day 52
For Me 53
Like an Ancestor 54
Prepping 55
Sunrise Service 57
Youth Dew 58
Mama Home? 59
Heroes 60
653-9218 61
Nursery Rhyme in Black 62
These Feet 63

ACKNOWLEDGMENTS 67
ABOUT THE AUTHOR 69

Foreword
Ariana Benson
author of Black Pastoral, winner of the Cave Canem Poetry Prize

My Mama moved among the days
like a dreamwalker in a field:
. . .
she got us almost through the high grass
then seemed like she turned around and ran
right back in
right back on in
—LUCILLE CLIFTON

As a collection of poems born of Black motherhood—the observation of it, the being daughtered by it, the becoming into it, the loss of it—Nursery Rhymes in Black is the hearty language child of so many cultural histories. It tends to the idiosyncratic truths lived by author Latorial Faison and her grandmother who raised her, a grand figure captured so vividly, so tenderly that the poem-character of her feels almost as familiar as she does unknowable; close enough for readers to watch the sweat forming like diamonds in the caves of her furrowed-over-stove brow, but with just enough of her out of frame, her fullness visible only to those who knew her in her time, in her world, as in the opening poem:

> She was a goodnight prayer, a moon that shined down through my bedroom window. She was the alphabet, a Sunday School verse, a third Sunday gospel song to rehearse, a mostly misunderstood exchange of power, responsibility & command.

If her Mama is a moon, Faison hangs her so fully in the sky of these poems, not shying away from some of her less beautiful beliefs, the craters in her well-worn surface. She casts lush images like so many twinkling stars whose luminance only emphasizes this matriarchal splendor, an imposing singularity in the black of night. Admittedly, many of the constellations conjured in her background are ones I recognize from my own childhood universe: the issues of the *Virginian Pilot* stacked on my grandmother's kitchen table, the shady 7-11 gas stations and knowing which ones were safest to fill up, Hancock Peanuts, boiled road-trip snack perfection. This collection rests upon poems of place, poems of a world whose inherent, architectural Blackness thrives in spite of, poems that guide readers (as did the stars the wise men) to their own promised land.

Much of the promise of *Nursery Rhymes in Black* lies in the way this collection reveals generational *knowing*; this is fitting, given that its titular mode of storytelling is one that so often uses rhythmic melody to blur an undercurrent of darker histories and meanings. If you already know the truths bound up in this book, the poems will vividly reanimate them. If you don't, read on to see them painstakingly unveiled. To begin to know what a Southern Black mother goes through, what she might be looking for at the bottom of a crystal tumbler or at the end of a verse. Know what it's like to "love / a white child to death" and "nurse a malnourished / Black one back to good / health with her poor, / dark, gifted self." Know what kind of *worsts* she prepares for, and where she keeps her checkbook for when they inevitably arrive. Know what it means to be a Black mother raised by a Black mother, and not know how to make sense of a world where this is no longer true.

In her *Lose Your Mother*, Black feminist scholar and cultural historian Saidiya Hartman writes: "Loss remakes you. Return is as much about the world to which you no longer belong as it is about the one in which you have yet to make a home." To lose your mother, then, is to have a part of you leave with her, and have the rest returned to a world in which you no longer belong. In poems like "A Whole Town's Eyes" and "How to Bury Your Mama" (excerpted below), the surreality of this grief lodges itself in the creases of everyday life, warping mundane ephemera into piercing reminders of absence:

> You look at all the people, all the pictures, all the things she wore
> & touched & you touch them, drape them all over you in hopes
> of feeling the warmth of her sun again. She is absolutely every-

where: in old sweaters, hairbrushes, pillow shams & in a black leather Sunday School change purse filled with bobby pins.

You still see her. Even in all the faces that are not hers, you see her trying to survive, trying to breathe, trying to find words, spirituals & hugs, motherless children, and God in this medium between Courtland & glory; you want to go with her.

. . .

In the days, months & years ahead, you hold on to every word she said like it was gospel because she was the only truth you ever knew; you know that now. You do not agree with death; you do not understand God.

By the time we reach "When We Fall on Our Knees," Faison's speaker has herself joined the choral *we* of Black motherhood and has thus gained new knowledges, new losses to fear those of her own children, of so many Black children this world would make motherless. It's enough to make anyone question God, the life laid out on these pages, enough to make anyone turn to Him for comfort anyway. The poems in this collection, then, forge ahead in the wake of this non-understanding, keeping close the memory-mementos of childhood life in Courtland—of lifelong holiday traditions and corner store excursions and whispered prayers—the speaker's mother in the background for all of it, her spirit a backdrop like the Black heavens against which the words here glow and burn.

At the same time, these poems, through Faison's dedicated framing and firm hand, sing with a choral awareness—knowing they are joined by many other voices in the harmony of Southern Black hymn-histories (in "Mama Sang the Blues").

Like whippoorwills, like Mama, and like every strong Black woman who came before me, I *come to this fountain . . . rich and sweet*. They come whistling. She comes singing. I come believing that we come to raise the dead.

These poems, in their pastel fascinators and satin-sheen stockings, turn to their neighbors in the literary pews (the resonant poems of writers like Lucille Clifton and Wanda Coleman spring first to mind), and ask *how you doin' sister so-and-so*, and in response, say *I'm blessed to see another morning*. They embody the role of church mother—a motherhood not designated by biology, but rather elder status and commitment to care of the youth, lest they fall to the wayside of this wretched world. They offer both a harsh word and a soft purse mint, sternness as guidance, sweetness as salve.

Anyone who's been to the church that Faison's mother so loved, the church that I grew up in, knows little more rouses a Sunday morning congregation like a good solo, brash and belted in a tone too singular to ever fully blend with her home section. Knows how the *let Him use yous* and the *take ya time, nows* shower down as the vocalist humbly reveals herself from the crowd of robed voices, expression as stoic as one who knows she's about to blow the roof off the sanctuary can stand to be. Knows the way the singer approaches the microphone, how she adjusts the stand and unfurls the cord a few lengths at her feet, is all part of the ritual of the performance. *Nursery Rhymes in Black* is a collection that understands so much of Blackness is this: a beautiful performance, one where the audience plays as key a role as any of those on the stage or at the pulpit. It's an inverted sort of collective theater in which the characters, after a long, hard week of playing the roles they must out in the white world, line the pews as audience and let their true selves shout and shine.

Giving Mama the solo means Faison has cast herself, in this collection, as choir director, a slightly less glamorous role on its face, but one without which there would be no song at all. I invite you reader, as you make your way through this Black lyric hymnal, to keep an eye on Faison's instructive poetic hands. How their movement staccatos when emphasis is needed. How a short poem ends abruptly with the quick swoop of a circled fist, leaving bated breath between its end and the next notes, ushered in with the come-hither of an astonishing first line, the kind that demands a new ear, a fresh eye. As you let the rhythms and cries of bellowing standouts "I'm So Courtland," "Mama Home?," "Important Papers," and "These Feet" (to name only a few of my personal favorites) use you, make of you a swaying devotee, throw yourself, reader, at the altar of these poems, the raw power of the stories within—and find yourself made anew, made whole again, after their final amen.

ARIANA BENSON is a Southern Black ecopoet born in Norfolk, Virginia, whose debut poetry collection, *Black Pastoral* (University of Georgia Press, 2023), won the 2022 Cave Canem Poetry Prize, the 2024 Lenore Marshall Poetry Prize from the Academy of American Poets, and the Kate Tufts Discovery Award, and was a finalist for the National Books Critics Circle Leonard Prize and the Library of Virginia Prize in Poetry. Benson is a recipient of a National Endowment for the Arts Fellowship, a Ruth Lilly and Dorothy Sargent Rosenberg Fellowship, and awards from The Poetry Foundation, Furious Flower, the Oak Spring Garden Foundation, the Porter House Review, and the 2021 Graybeal-Gowen Prize for Virginia Poets. Her poems and essays have appeared in *Ploughshares*, *The Yale Review*, *The Kenyon Review*, *Poetry Magazine*, Poem-a-day, and elsewhere. Benson is a proud alumna of Spelman College, where she facilitates creative writing and storytelling workshops for HBCU students.

NURSERY RHYMES IN BLACK

She who gives love
must learn to organize pain.

Mama Was a Negro Spiritual

She was a goodnight prayer, a moon that shined down through my bedroom window. She was the alphabet, a Sunday School verse, a third Sunday gospel song to rehearse, a mostly misunderstood exchange of power, responsibility & command.

She was a black '73 Ford LTD, a Nottoway River crossing, a house filled with too many other folks' children, an orphan that life and death left behind to find, to give, some joy. She was a funeral-going, everybody-in-Southampton-County-knowing, bad-manner-destroying pillar of strength.

She was a Friday evening ride to town, a Saturday morning cleaning, a Sunday go-to-meeting kind of human being. She laughed louder than Jim Crow's law & cried softer than God's peace.

She was the secret I never told, the carrying of some other man and woman's burden. She was rare, uncut, Black & picked up, ripped from some earthen mine, placed beneath a sharecropper's kind to bear witness, to bear it all deep down inside.

She was a black hearse, a def man walking, a raising & waving of tired hands; she was thunder; she was lightning, a heavy rain that fell in spring. She was a third-grade education, small-town syndication, her house a good book & she the words penned fervently, permanently on all its pages.

She was a Ridley Road scholar, a kitchen where cooking got done & well; she was Ms. Shirley, the lunch lady, bus driver, Sammy's wife, giver of too much self. Mama was a Negro spiritual, a hymn hummed from inside a Baptist Hymnal, in an old rocking chair from a corner of our living room.

She was a wisdom no man could whistle, a fancy no woman could fake, a journey none living in the now could take. She was an old-fashioned lyric everybody could lift their voice and sing.

Witness

When I see yellow school buses,
I think of the late 1970s & Mama—

the hard-working black woman she was
giving black life to whatever all life
needed.

I think of all the boys & girls
—white with character lunchboxes in their hands,
mommies & daddies to go with them.

White child center
stage, black child a
witness.

History Woman

It was a dying womb
where she came from,
dreaming of a life
in Norfolk & new shoes,
a place to call her own
a clean room.

Orphaned, she was
grateful for a little life
hers & mine, that God
cared enough to make
room in a house
without a welcome mat
in a world where she
was too black & too big
for the opportunities of white folk.

But she could cook
& clean; she could love
a white child to death
nurse a malnourished
Black one back to good
health with her poor,
dark, gifted self.

She knew it all—
about tobacco leaves
sol'ja beans, cotton fields
& seasonin' greens.

When she fried her
fish & baked her
famous cobbler dish,
it was genius
how she always made
sugar from shit.

I Am Not Ashamed of Your Gospel

We are connected, henceforth &
forevermore by irons binding our fathers &
mothers, stowed away in the darkness of a
slave ship, bought & sold by an evil
that still sells all of this.

We are kindred spirits kindling spiritual fires,
bearing, somehow, pain, summoning,
somehow, hope, writing what angels have
tried to spell, what root doctors have tried to
heal & reverse, what white historians have
dispelled to rehearse.

Descending on all kinds of division,
multiplying every protest, adding to us power,
we are ones,
the only ones, all the ones we have ever waited for.

You wrote the blessed words; you led the sad
songs, penned the she psalms, all the prayers of
Black women you prayed them, anointed oil that
blessed our pages through pain.

Together we have been lonely & alone, a proverb
dripping from a wall pipe in the stillness of the
cold, the death of the night; you cried freedom
from your womb for ours.

I am not ashamed of your gospel, for it is black
& female & powerful—an education we need,
a hymnal from which we sing, the hope God
gave for all the colored girls to save.

Self-Portrait

My birth chart reveals a stone—
forty-five, strong-willed, creative & free

I look into a mirror & there she is—
young mother wrapping me in swaddling clothes

Handing me to a higher calling
like a Black baby Jesus

I look closer—outside, I see one mother
inside another

I am their battle cry; they have anointed my head
with their oils

In a different lifetime—I am these
women with the same kind of man

Same kind of children
same kind of heart

Same kind of white folk
same kind of god.

Mama Sang the Blues

Mama's bottle tested illusion. Therein was holy water from a great river that healed the sick and raised the dead. She sipped small sips with her black lips, hummed hymns nice and slow, in and out of contralto, like Mahalia Jackson.

Tell the angels, she'd sing—*that I'm on my way*, toe-tapping, head-rocking, hardworking, poor, and saved. Bittersweet like a one-room school, she came together without academic tools; she was heaven-sent. The god of white evil couldn't create a Black woman like this.

Like a daystar, she appeared in indigo skies, orphaned and unknown. From a dying womb to a tenant room, she came like a blonde-haired, blue-eyed baby Jesus in a brown-skinned country—*it didn't make no sense.*

The poison she picked, it was a balm that chased evil, from lying tongues to the lynching of sons. Mama grew stronger than Samson on a Friday night when she slipped away to steal her humanity back.

It was a happy sadness that dealt in pain, one I never heard her name or give claim. For when the white folk got your tongue, you can't talk to nobody but Jesus, and when Jesus got you singing like Mahalia, you can't trust nobody but God.

Mama was serious about religion, the Baptist church down the dirt road, and choir rehearsals on Tuesday nights. With songbooks, handwritten lyrics, and a third-grade education, she impressed her own self. Standing in that choir on the promises of God, all robed and righteous, she was worth more than white women.

Her voice, like a whippoorwill, could whistle and sing all through the night, all through the struggle, all through the pain, all through the blackness of being dead and alive. When she sang from her darkness, I knew she was light.

Mama was a voice of dark brown reason—calling out to God, crying out from Earth. What can wash away my sin, *what can make me whole again* . . . I listened with everything that had come between us.

She helped turn me into me with a melody she had sewn together through all kinds of hell. *O precious is thy flow that makes me white as snow* . . . Mama was an instrument inhaling grief, exhaling peace of mind, a piece of mine. She was a professor of arts and letters, and God quilting me with all the pieces she was.

Like whippoorwills, like Mama, and like every strong Black woman who came before me, I *come to this fountain . . . rich and sweet.* They come whistling. She comes singing. I come believing that we come to raise the dead.

Sundays

  Sundays stayed holy
singin' cookin' worshippin'
  God in those Black hands.

Fast Girls

Mama always said this about fast girls,
that they were faster than butter runnin' down
a hot knife. Everything done in the dark will
sho nuf come to the light, and it don't take long either.

And for hangin' out at night, Mama said ain't nothing
good goin' on in the streets but stuff to be ashamed of
later on in life, like teenage girls poppin' their coattails
to men old enough to be their granddaddies and boys
hustlin' dope and makin' babies before they themselves
become men. Naw, there ain' nothin good happenin'
after twelve o'clock when everybody should be asleep
in their own house with they own folks.

But fast girls, they like to come home in the morning bringing early
babies with late daddies. That's what Momma always said,
ain' no need in rushin' life cause we ain' gone
do no more than the good Lord wants us to.

Abominations

Mama said this about bulldaggers:
they were *shame n' scandal*
something to carry down in history.

She'd grab my little hand, hurry on by
like the lesbianism
somehow

I'd inhale it—
get it in my central nervous
system and die.

Young's Literal Translation

Mama lived vicariously
through *Tidewaters News*,
The Virginian Pilot,
and every word of God.

She believed
Luke seventeen and two,
For it is the gospel.
She pictured it—

Her poor, Black self
drowning in the Nottoway River
Millstone about her neck,
Father, Son, and Holy Ghost.

I Know It Was the Blood

> *I know it was the blood,*
I know it was the blood,
> *I know it was the blood saved me.*

It was a holy communion
> beneath a steeple of Black womanhood
clothed in the full armor of God.

All the women at the church wore white:
> white dresses, white suits, white gloves,
white pearls & white hats.

For nearly twenty years,
> I watched Mama 'nem do this
in *remembrance of Him*.

They took bread & ate it,
> they took wine & drank it,
they went out into their own Mount of Olives.

Mama hated when a woman wore white with anything black
underneath:
> bra, panties, girdle, slip, panty hose;
she said it made everything look dingy.

> *One day when I was lost,*
she died on a cross,
> *I know it was the blood saved me.*

Hallelujah Anyhow

Mama drove a yellow school bus, cooked in school cafeterias
& cleaned white folk's houses. Daddy cleaned their yards,

Worked their farms, drove nails in their boards, built their
Houses, their schools, their churches, their office buildings,

Their grocery & department stores. They came home each
Day to a four-turned-eight-room house that took thirty years

To pay for, a house they worked hard to make a home—
For me & every child who ever laid their head down in it,

Every child they raised from something dead. They knew
Black America like the backs of their hands, that it was

A hallelujah *anyhow*, a dice game, a juke joint, a song they
Danced, a come-to-Jesus moment; it was more than

What they had yesterday. Life had been scattered
With hope for what a tomorrow could bring. They knew

White America was no Black man's promised land,
But they got out of bed every day anyhow, pressed on

For whatever victory they had in that white Jesus
Hanging high in a picture framed—in their living room.

They kept the faith because in America, life could
Change for the better in a Southampton County minute,

A shotgun marriage, an out-of-wedlock birth, at a funeral,
With a graduation, in an old white woman's kitchen,

Or the tilling of a white man's fields. There rested
A promise that hard work paid, not well, but good

Enough to raise boys & girls America might one day
Call sons & daughters, men & women, Black or White,

Rich or poor—American. Their Black lives mattered,
To them—to them first, to them most of all.

Our Town

In the old Jerusalem, the memories baptize us. Across the bridge & just beyond the stoplight a history that has maimed us lies.

A courthouse of antebellum icons & secrets: a rebel slave's sword, a Confederate statue, a Nottoway River black & running somewhere from something.

Off Main Street, a hanging tree once stood—where Negro preacher & slave revolt leader Nat Turner became another strange fruit.

Like three blind mice, three white churches stand watch covering blood shed by white hoods: one for their fathers, one for their sons, one for their holy ghosts.

The Walter Cecil Rawls Library & Museum sitting afar off & beneath the trees hidden, like so much of the truth.

Shands—where the upper-middle-class white kids lived—where Mama was handpicked to drive their bus to public school post-segregation.

The 7-11 where a white clerk called the police on Mama for pumping more than $10 worth of gas & Officer Bass showed up summonsed her to the Courtland Jail.

The Southampton County Courthouse with the large white columns where Mama's case, unlike Nat Turner's & so many other enslaved Negroes, was dismissed.

What used to be Thompson's Restaurant, Danny's & Mama Joe's, where, rumor has it, a Black man had been killed for going with a white woman.

Pine Haven—where both my grandmas, at some point in their black lives, worked in white folk's houses.

The railroad tracks separating U.S. mail & county jail, Black & white, poverty & wealth, town & country, outhouses & indoor toilets, pump wells & running water.

Southampton Academy, brainchild of *the resistance*—300 whites who signed a petition protesting integrated education & mixing their kids with *niggers*.

58 East to Franklin, Southampton Memorial Hospital, Union Camp paper mill, a Kentucky Fried Chicken & High's Ice Cream,

58 West to Emporia, Hancock Peanuts & the middle school, the once segregated Black high school known as Riverview & Southampton County Training School.

Courtland—if the landmarks & country stores don't tell the whole truth all, the road signs will of *hanging trees, blackhead signposts*, good ole' boys & slave rebellion.

I'm So Courtland

I'm so Courtland I remember ... Daddy buying me bubble-gum cigars at Marion Joyner's store, getting my hair pressed & curled at *Mrs. Emma Lou's*, getting $10 physicals at Dr. Daughtry's, and buying grape icebergs from Mrs. Wilson next to what used to be the old Riverview High School for Blacks.

I'm so Courtland, I remember walking to Ms. Inell Scott's house when in the town to get an oatmeal pie, playing softball on the hill at Mrs. Sarah Lee's, making too many trips to Engram's Funeral Home— because Mama knew everybody who died & wanted to view their bodies, pay her respects.

I'm so Courtland, I remember going to my Grandma Earline's yard parties down the road, and having Mama & Daddy's friend Mrs. Inell read my palm when she visited only to smile & say, *Shelly, there ain' no work in these hands.*

I'm so Courtland, I remember Mr. Perry letting us into Friday night football games for free, being excited to see the Rollins man coming who sold everything out of the back of a Volvo station wagon, especially those big peppermint sticks that lasted for days, and walking through the cornfield to Flowers' store.

I'm so Courtland, I remember getting one hundred pieces of penny candy or cookies for one dollar and the best ham or BLT sandwiches at cousin Tanky Boy's Star on the Roof where Mama also had us work during summers for five dollars a day and free meals.

I'm so Courtland, I remember attending Kitchen Butts' family reunions every Fourth of July, being able to hear the SHS marching band's infamous beats while playing in the backyard, and of course ... no child *ever* turning down a trip to the nearby city of Franklin.

Forbidden Fruit

In the '80s, we dressed up in costumes. Mama took us into town to the Courtland Rec. It was Halloween.

Inside, kids were bobbing for apples, and I in my Wonder Woman costume did not feel strong enough to put my lips into a tub of water where all the kids had bobbed & slobbed.

It seemed as though every Black child in Courtland had come to celebrate yet another holiday white folks had made, but weren't we entitled.

Just like with Eden, just like with Adam. Just like with Eve, I was surrounded by words on pages translated by white men.

So Christmas and Easter have somehow become just like Halloween—and bobbing for apples.

Important Papers

When I see GoFundMe pages for funerals, I think of Mama & all the lessons she taught. The first thing I wonder is why so many die without life insurance, why nobody prepared. Didn't they have grandparents with side hustles, some know-how, some get-up-and-go?

Didn't they have a grandma with a bank bag & a checkbook? Truth is, everybody didn't get it, the same lesson I got, from my Black grandma who only went about as high as the eighth grade, who cooked in school cafeterias, drove school buses & worked part-time in white folk's houses?

Two Saturdays out of every month we had a visitor, the insurance man—or the insurance woman. Mama would send me to get the insurance books she kept wrapped in plastic bags inside a zippered faux leather bank bag in a dresser drawer of important papers in her bedroom—books of policies, coupons & receipts for six to eight dollars.

Mama had policies on everybody: herself, Daddy, every child in the house. She even had policies for the grown children who weren't really grown. Mama didn't believe in not having enough, not preparing enough, not preparing a place for a rainy day—emergencies, sickness, disease & death.

Every month Mrs. Dolly Goodwyn or a white man named Mr. Bobby Harrell—dressed in his Sunday best—would come collecting the insurance payments. They sat in our den on a sofa Mama only uncovered for company. They made small talk while Mama let me write the checks for the insurance payments.

Mama would sign the check. I'd take the insurance books, put them back in the plastic bag, back into the bank bag, back into her bedroom dresser drawer where Mama kept all of her important papers, house notes & bank books.

I learned that Mama knew business, that Mama took care of her business, that Black people, even if we were poor, needed to know about & have important papers. If a son or daughter, grandchild, or foster child ever died, Mama had a policy.

Mama had learned a long time ago, & she taught it to me, that even if we must scuffle, even if we must struggle, from the day we are born to the day we die, we must prepare a place & find a way to go fund ourselves.

Girl, 1983

after Jamaica Kincaid

Listen. Obey your parents in the Lord *for this is right.* Go to school, be good, and respect grown folk. You hear me? Honor your mother and your father *so your days will be longer on this Earth.* Trust God. Go to church and Sunday school and Bible study and choir rehearsal, sing the songs, read the scriptures, say yes ma'am and no sir when folk talking to you. You hear me? Hold your head up and look at folk in the eyes when they talking to you. Don't be sassy and grown. I can't stand no grown child. And don't wear no halter tops, and don't you ever let me catch you sitting in no grown man's lap. Use your manners. You hear me? Act like I been raising you right. Don't eat in other folk's houses; act like I fed you before we left home. Act like you been raised, like you got some home training. And don't be sassing no white man and woman; they can make it hard. But don't let em' think you stupid either. I ain't raising no fool. You hear me? If anybody ever touch you down there, you better tell me. Don't be no fast girl; ain't nothing out there in them streets but babies and trouble; the last thing I need is a crying baby. If you make it, you gon' rock it. So keep—yo—legs—*closed*; speak proper like I sent you to school. And use good English. You hear me? Put a dress on when you go up there on that stage, and don't be walking like no boy. Respect old folk and you will live a long time. Be clean. Be mannerable. Be thankful; appreciate what you got. Treat people right. Be kind to children; you never know which one of them might have to give you your last glass of water 'for you die. Trust God; he ain't *never* failed me yet. You hear me? God will *never leave you nor forsake you.* You hear me? Have some respect, and don't you give me no backtalk. Pick your feet up in this house. Don't be trifling; don't be sorry; don't be like the rest of 'em. You be you. Be different. *Charity starts at home.* GIVE YOUR LIFE TO GOD! You hear me? Don't you follow no crowd. If you bring a baby in this house, it's gon' be *Katy bar the door. All them boys want is to keep your belly taut as a tick, and that will be the end of you 'cause they ain' gon' hit a lick at black snake and ain' got a pot to piss in or a window to throw it out. You hear me? Stay in school. Get your homework out. Make good grades, and listen to them teachers. You got to be smart. Stay with God. He will not lead you wrong. Jesus will carry you through.*

When We Fall on Our Knees

Black mothers pray another way
sometimes in other languages.

We pray over & for our Black sons
calling on the ancestors to guide us,

To give them the strength to climb,
the same strength they rose up with,

Survived slave ships & plantation strife,
to face the lynching, to steal away

To a Jesus in the night. We kneel down
to say how and why a *yessir* be a holy

Word—on the street, down a country
road, at a traffic light, in the middle

Of the night, massah translated into sir,
missus translated into ma'am, a white woman

Weaponizing whiteness for Black pain,
claiming you be a threat to all her things,

White masculinity, white woman fragility
when all you want to do is dream a dream,

When all we really want them to do is breathe
another way, another day, in another

Language, we pray over & for Black boys
in the names of Black fathers, Black sons,

Black holy ghost ones—spirits that dwell
in the deep, caught between Africa & America,

Confederacy & Union, between these knees
& jail, between their future & their last exhale.

Judas Kiss

Sleeping in Black man-caves alone & silenced like
Hogs tied to slaughter at birth, eyes
wide shut by un-holy un-Black people with
money poison & guns uniformed daily
daily unveiled we sing praises while we hug while
we forgive this white America wipe away
the shame Judas-kiss ourselves to hell all righteous forsaken.

Black and Forth

Dead & gone like King
Like Malcolm, like Obama
We be a Black dream
We be a Black dream
Like 40 acres & mules
Like the right to love

Like the right to love
We be craving honey, house
Sometimes without home
Sometimes without home
We be craving all the world
Like the right to vote

Like the right to vote
We dared to dream, learned to read
Like Phillis, the Bible
Like Phillis, the Bible
Bearing white people's myths, gifts
On the wings of words

On the wings of words
Black men & Black women flew
From slavery to freedom
From slavery to freedom
Our enslaved people survived
The whip & the chains

The whip & the chains
O how they tried to break us
For America
For America
The colonies our backs built
Betrayed & traded

Betrayed & traded
Like lambs led to a slaughter
We be fatted calves
We be fatted calves
Sacrificed at the return
Of wayward children

Of wayward children
America calls not things
As though they are here
As though they are here
America calls not things
Of wayward children

Of wayward children
Sacrificed at the return
We be fatted calves
We be fatted calves
Like lambs led to a slaughter
Betrayed & traded

Betrayed & traded
The colonies our backs built
For America
For America
O how they tried to break us
The whip & the chains

The whip & the chains
Our enslaved people survived
From slave to freedom
From slave to freedom
Black men & Black women flew
On the wings of words

On the wings of words
Bearing white people's myths, gifts
Like Phillis, the Bible
Like Phillis, the Bible
We dared to dream, learned to read
Like the right to vote

Like the right to vote
We be craving all the world
Sometimes without home
Sometimes without home
We be craving honey, house
Like the right to love

Like the right to love
Like 40 acres & mules
We be a black dream
We be a black dream
Like Malcolm, like Obama
Dead & gone like King.

Testify

Somebody help me
     come forward—
to recite the blessing,
     to sing the violence,
to pray tell that it's not
     real.
For this is the saddest
     funeral;
these are the worst
     of times
& we look so happy
     dying.

Where Is God?

When they kill
       innocent Black
              boys
      when Earth

is emptied

when moons
      wane
             when suns
    are eclipsed

when world
    spins off axis
         with all the rage

with all the cunning
    all the coonin'
        all the back & forth
  'til somebody

or something
        dies?

When a Monarch Dies

When a monarch dies, Black & Brown responses
reveal a truth unrelenting

The evils of colonization, the chains of slavery,
systemic oppression—be wounds that never heal.

Every day a new lynching because every day a new clinching
of crown jewels & pearls—looted, pillaged, stolen.

We witness all the sadness, sing all the blues
seeking sanctity & sanity, sovereignty & savior

When a monarch: a Black man, a Black woman,
a Black boy, a Black girl dies

The whole world is forced to bear a nobler truth:
a greatest lie ever told—a love that never wins.

Heaven

There ain' no heaven opening up here, except the heaven we open up for ourselves. Women have spent entire lifetimes opening up heavens for men who thought they gave us the world:

A helping hand, a kind word, an education, a proclamation, a constitution. Women have paved streets with their gold, painted wings on angels & let men call them cherubim, seraphim.

Women have sat beneath the thrones they gave way to, settled for uncrowned, uncircumcised jewels & stolen nations.

Women have birthed babies, loved & unloved, wanted & unwanted, cast them into dust & spells, early graves & early morning light.

Women have opened up so many heavens, every heaven, all the heavens except their own; we have not shown ourselves the light, our light.

We must baptize ourselves in the holy ghost that is woman, be all things holy, all things heavenly to ourselves.

This Place

I have come to a place
where the only white people I understand

are the ones who have come
to understand me

in this place—where a Mamie Till is still
bent, broken, barren & grieving

where I am a pallbearer
carrying what remains

of innocent Black boys
somewhere

somehow
to some other American grave.

The Un-Praised

They raise their right hands, believe in God
       & not just the one they have to dismantle.

They raise up children & believe in afterlife,
       pro-life & pro-choice, that heaven is a safehouse.

They raise Black men from so much dead with
       ugly truths; they believe hell is a real world, this one.

They raise spirits & drink spirits to believe in a love
       this world has lied about from sanctified spaces.

They believe in little fingers & toes, that they be the
       little g's, the lost gods recruiting humans for being.

She Who Gives Love

Slayed in a riverbed, captive
By the art of revolution, beauty draped

Across jagged edged sword severing
Other men's souls.

Sun and moon lie about it all
Every thing of wonder in orbit

Inner cry, a range of mountains
Sometimes death.

Try them on with grace
Cast them off with clarity.

She who gives love
Must learn to organize pain.

Outside the Picture Window

        What was *is*
you left in September.

        It took three months
instead of five.

        You saw God
outside the picture window.

        He smiles with you,
He cried with me

        'Til I grew numb,
'til you grew cold.

        You disappeared
in a cloud,

        A big black car,
I wrote it down inside.

        I remember,
Your heart stopped.

        My heart dropped,
you died.

A Whole Town's Eyes

It was an escape
    this death.

How could you leave
    the business of my blood undone?

Irreconciled, incomplete
    nothing,

A void to fill
    with words, hearsay, daydreams,

A whole town's
    eyes.

How to Bury Your Mama

You take her hands in yours & you bury them beneath the white sheet that covers her face & yours. You watch her strong Black body slide into the back of a black hearse parked in the grass of her frontyard outside the picture window she cleaned for 35 years, your whole life.

You go back into the house & stare at all the empty spaces she once filled: the kitchen where soul food was cooked every single day. Dumplings, cobblers, collard greens, banana puddings, pies & homemade rolls—never to be made again.

You stand in the bedroom where the mirror's edge is decorated all around with pictures of you & your family, where the scent in the curtains she ordered from Sears has instantly increased their worth by millions.

You sit in her old wooden chair with the pillow for a cushion & read every letter you wrote to her; you see all the pictures of happy moments you shared, Christmas & birthday cards, your first book—all tucked away in a drawer like stacks of cash she was setting aside for tough times.

You peruse the obituaries of family & friends, grandparents, great aunts & uncles, piled neatly signifying Black death & Black grief, Black love & Black wealth, the best & saddest funeral songs & soloists, a circle of life documenting history, a Black library.

You look at your Daddy, 89 with Alzheimer's, trying to figure out where she is, why Engram's boy took her away in that black car of his because she is not dead, where they laid her & you wish, for a moment, that you could not remember, like him.

You remember the old folk & the Bible saying how quickly we would all be changed. "In the twinkle of an eye," she left the house in a wind that blew, her last breath.

You look at all the people, all the pictures, all the things she wore & touched & you touch them, drape them all over you in hopes of feeling the warmth of her sun again. She is absolutely everywhere: in old sweaters, hairbrushes, pillow shams & in a black leather Sunday School change purse filled with bobby pins.

You still see her. Even in all the faces that are not hers, you see her trying to survive, trying to breathe, trying to find words, spirituals & hugs, motherless children, and God in this medium between Courtland & glory; you want to go with her.

You plan a home going. You decide what & who is good enough to display her worth, to say the right words, to play the right music, to sing the right songs by which men, women, children & a whole community will remember her forever.

You sit in a Black church because a Black church is who she was & you watch people pass by you to view what little remains.

You imagine she is somewhere with two wings flying high among angels, singing gospel, cooking & taking care of all the dead children who got their wings too soon, smiling in a heaven as you sit all bereaved & broken trying to exegete scripture, to decipher God—wishing she would just walk in, that it is all a dream, that she is the Lord's next big miracle to be raised from the dead at Shiloh.

You are declared numb, stung by the sting of cancer, left behind with too much to bear, people she loved who, two by two, march behind clergy & casket to a grave she bought, for she believed in preparing a place for her own self.

You melt as the Black preacher speaking blessings over the living & the dead pours ashes that are not hers into a grave that is; you wish everything you ever learned about death was a lie.

In the days, months & years ahead, you hold on to every word she said like it was gospel because she was the only truth you ever knew; you know that now. You do not agree with death; you do not understand God.

You take her hands in yours & you bury them beneath pain, sorrow & tears, beneath an undertaker's white sheet that covers all while you never quite recover at all.

The Last Easter

   Black & woman
you always rose again.

   There was no coming down
from your cross

   only to carry it:
disciples, crown of thorns, sepulcher & all

   a whole cloud of witnesses weeping
believing in your miracle

   tongues of fire praying
to you prayers

   a whole world bearing witness
to the power

   of your last supper
the raising of yourself from so much dead.

Tribulation

Southern White upbringing Black as Mama ever was
in a little Black church down an old country road

with a cinder-block pool for a baptism
might be all I ever needed to know about life, about Black and White

of America and Jesus—woven, painted & drilled into the bread,
the wine, the communion gloves, the white table linens

I have given to this life, a man child three times—an Eve in Eden
biting apples, giving Adams up to dust, to lust, to die for this blood

hanging from a Calvary—crucified, dying & rising again daily
Godchild God sent, unfed, unwed, un-bled, undone

deliver me from sin, from Black-white church,
from steeples, from people, from myself

A Shroud for Mother's Day

It takes twenty-four hours to grieve a mother's—day gone wrong after twenty-one years of finger-painted hands on pastels, four-year-old faces peeking from the center of my world & die-cut flowers in preschool gardens. It takes twenty-four hours to grieve a mother's day gone wrong without human touch, a *hey mom*, or hug, not an egg scrambled with cheese or love. It takes twenty-four hours to grieve a mother's day gone without my not so grown but gone sons who breathe this air I gave—like it's a free for all, like it's free—to all, like it's—free. It takes me twenty-four hours to grieve a mother's day gone wrong, nobody I gave life—stopping to remember what I stopped living for.

For Me

On my mind
    always
you were there
when I couldn't think
    for me
never forgetting
the life, the love
    the lessons
the joy of Sundays
late-night talk
    of country folk
mishaps and misfortunes
how you prayed
    for me
to be somebody's woman
late to bed, early
    to rise
your hands at hard labor
kneading dough, turning
    wheels
cooking meals
for eating
    for teaching
for me.

Like an Ancestor

Like an ancestor we never knew, your smile shined with Southern sun's warmth. Your hands, like honeybees, were always busy as a city street, quiet as a country road coming together, making memories & all the good times real.

Your lips outlined a kind vernacular; a beauty lived in the lining of your tongue every time we laid eyes & ears on you—you never did grow old. With wisdom, style & common sense, you gave life.

Like oceans bearing in the tide, you came gathering life, giving life, praising God, every day bearing witness to storms, breaking ground, changing climate, whispering secrets to winds, taking everyone with you, leaving us, somehow—renewed.

Prepping

Mama would buy all the local stores out of toilet paper, paper towels, navy beans, black-eyed peas, sugar, bleach, powdered milk & ammonia. She would have had my foster brothers & me filling up old milk gallon jugs with water & storing them in the crawl space beneath the house.

Mama would make us wash our hands all day & night religiously, all ritual-like, before breakfast, before & after touching anybody anywhere & anything, especially of hers & again before bed so you couldn't infect anybody in your wildest dreams.

Mama was the kind of Black woman who knew too much about cleanliness; she didn't let just anybody inside our house. Some folks she talked to from the top of the stoop. Just like TB, the AIDS, syphilis & gonorrhea, she didn't want stomach flu, bird flu, nobody's flu virus in her house & didn't much care how it got spread. To keep clean, she killed everything stinking, rotten, filthy & even *black*.

Mama had learned to wipe down a house like she had learned to clean a chicken bone or a fish bone—with precision & skill, leaving no meat & nothing behind. When Mama told you to stay out of somebody's house, she meant it & you had better pay attention. She didn't want nobody bringing roaches, fleas & chinches back home.

In Mama's book, cleanliness wasn't *next to* godliness; it *was* godliness. Her bottom line was zero—zero dirt. She didn't have much, but what she had, she had worked too damn hard to get it & keep it. Mama wasn't a G, but she prepped like one—always preparing for the end of the world. COVID-19, she would have given pure hell.

Sunrise Service

For as long as Mama lived
there had always been an Easter Sunday
morning in a Black church.

Pink, yellow, magenta & teal dresses
matching hair ribbons, Shirley Temple curls
five & dime store barrettes

Black patent leather shoes, bobby socks,
sunrise service with sausage, eggs, grits, bacon, or ham
that somebody like Mama, Mr. Will-B, or Mrs. Emma Lou cooked

Sunday school & staring at my reflection
in my black patent leather shoes—
the prettiest things I thought I ever owned

The Savior was risen, the food was blessed
We all ate, drank & went out into our own
Mount of Olives again.

Youth Dew

   She powdered her brown cheeks
& sang hymns,
    every day went out into her own
Mount of Olives.

   When she wasn't singing
her gospel,
    she was commanding us,
teaching us

   To honor our mothers
and our fathers
    so our days could be longer
upon the earth.

   She was always busy
making bread, making ends meet.
    I was always bewildered
by it all

   Like the strong stench
of her Estee Lauder Youth Dew,
    she'd *stay* with you
long after she was gone.

Mama Home?

I don't want to lose sight of
the strong woman who was *you*
the pride you took in being hard working,
forever helping, not wasting a piece of food
anything homemade or handed down
how you kept a clean house
and ran a tight ship
how 4 o'clock felt like a new day
because you were home
talking to your inner circle about outer circles
cooking baked chicken, fried fish,
fruit cobbler or some other *to-die-for* dish
listening to you was like watching
Esther Rolle movie episodes, *good times*
like reading Hurston's dialect-filled
oral histories, stories & rhymes
you were a southern female, Blackness
that got *real* proper when strangers called

I hear you in new ringtones that ring like
old phones, in soft voices like your friend
Emma Lou's asking, saying *Mama Home.*

I see you sitting there
half opened, half read *Tidewater News*
or *Virginian Pilot* in your tired hands
watching the 6 o'clock news
catching a nod or two
as 11 o'clock news watches you
in your favorite rocking chair.

Heroes

        When the earthly grow tired,
they just leave.

        So before you let them kiss you,
watch them tie their shoes.

        What makes us legend
is not chiseled in a stone.

        Heroes are only as good as
the sanctuary they give.

653-9218

For the first time in my thirty-nine
I dialed & nobody answered, not even God.

A classic had been read, closed, shelved,
—the end.

But I recall their strength, their country-strong voices:
the laughter, their surprise, their struggle, their sorrow,

their resilience, their church songs & field hands
—a building up with two by fours, their heating of pots & pans.

Theirs was an old-fashioned prayer
that kept me.

An era has ended,
the best of Sunday dinners no more.

Six, five, three—nine, two, one, eight
disconnected, gone, fate.

Nursery Rhyme in Black

       Remember the darker brother—stripped from a canvas in the
          cosmos,
surviving halfway in halfway houses: half-alive, half-gone, half-wed,
half-white,
          half-dead.

       Dropped from sky to count what never adds up,
just us tending to the live roots
          of every lynching tree.

       Never completely in or out of galaxy, in our out-of-
          their-right minds
half-true, half-false—like a cow jumping over the moon, like a slave
master's Jesus
          coming back real soon.

These Feet

These feet have been born. These feet have baby-walked the floor and through the doors of a four-room house that Mama & Daddy bought. These feet have been tickled and touched and loved. These feet have seen the ground of an outhouse, stood next to a slop jar. These feet have been, for generations, steadied, readied, stood upon, talked about, and taught how to walk through a thing, a dark thing, a light thing, an opened door.

These feet have learned to let me fall where I may, to pick me up when I cannot stay. These feet have learned to feel hurt, fail, and try again. These feet have known baby fat and Stride Rites in reds, whites, and blues. These feet have been kissed by their elders and ancestors, grandmothers and grandfathers, aunts and uncles, superstitious wellwishers, gurus and giants, the blood and the un-blood.

These feet have been led through post–Jim Crow in the South, Southampton County schools, and through the slow integration of a Southern town. These feet have walked the aisles of an old church, sat me down in an old wooden pew with a Sunday School book in my hand. These feet have stood before preachers, deacons and trustees, church mothers and members reciting scripture, poems, prayers and singing songs.

These feet have been blessed by elders, prayed over and prayed through a coup of generational curses. These feet have been to the pool, baptized in the name of the Father, the Son, and the Holy Ghost. These feet have stomped through house and home in search of heaven, running from hell. These feet have trusted God and man to carry them over, under, further, and through. These feet have found room at a cross, crossed over into a glory, and stood at the crossroads of all kinds of emancipation and new freedoms.

These feet have stood in Grandma and Granddaddy's house ready to draw water from the well, run through the front door, the kitchen where the biscuits were, and out the back door to the old farmland. These feet have known rivers like the Nottoway and all the Black Brown tears folk cried walking the road to freedom here.

These feet have waged war with their toes, broken down barriers with their soles. These feet cannot fail. These feet *have not failed me yet*. These feet have known joy and pain, the blessing of Black teachers, the curse of white bottom feeders.

These feet have walked halls of institutions once segregated, still segregated if truth be told. These feet have stood at the feet of those breaking bread and bearing good news These feet have stood at altars, sat down on a mourner's bench at a church revival. These feet have come to Jesus. These feet have had opportunities—too many to tell. These feet have caught tears, healed wounds, pulled a soul from the pit of hell.

These feet have lifted me up, brought me to myself time & time again. These feet know that Black feet matter, that Black feet have been stopped dead in their tracks, shot in their backs—with the whitest of lies. These feet have been chosen. These feet have born burdens, been a blessing, and brought good news.

These feet have been loved and in love with a boy, with a man, with a soul, with a spirit that comes upon me like consuming fire. These feet have been kissed with the tenderness of dew. These feet have never told it all. These feet have touched their soul's mate & made him whole. These feet have brought bond, matrimony, justice, and sons into the world. These feet have been called.

These feet have helped whomever they could wherever they could. These feet have stood for something, good through evil—on platforms small and wide. These feet have listened to and waited on God.

These feet have stood watch without moving, without being moved, never letting go, never losing sight, never losing ground, always gaining. Praise these feet who get up daily to meet their fate with brain, bowels, and bone. These feet have raised me from the dead. Praise these feet.

Praise God for these feet, these tired feet, these hired feet, these inspired feet, these justified feet, these feet, they keep finding their way, pressing their way. These feet keep leading the way home.

Acknowledgments

This collection has been shortlisted or ranked as finalist for the following:

    The Cave Canem Poetry Prize
    The Hudson Prize, Black Lawrence Press
    The Louise Bogan Poetry Award, Trio House Press
    The Trio House Press Open Reading Series
    Sundress Publications

The following poems were selected for the following publications in original or edited versions:

    "Black and Forth," *Penumbra*
    "Fast Girls," *L'Attitude* & *To Earth from Venus*, Virginia Tech
    "Hallelujah Anyhow," *Aunt Chloe*
    "How to Bury Your Mama," *Typehouse Literary Journal*
    "Judas Kiss," *Artemis Journal*
    "Like an Ancestor," *African Voices*
    "Mama Sang the Blues," *Penumbra*
    "Mama Was a Negro Spiritual," *Southern Poetry Anthology, vol. 9: Virginia*; *Winning Writers*; Tom Howard Poetry Prize Winner; *Crab Orchard Review*; Furious Flower Inaugural Gwendolyn Brooks Prize Semifinalist
    "Nursery Rhyme in Black," *Rhino* Founders Prize Finalist
    "Our Town," as "Courtland" in *Obsidian: Literature and Art in the African Diaspora*
    "A Shroud for Mother's Day," *Prairie Schooner*
    "653-9218," *Deep South Magazine*
    "Sundays," *Aunt Chloe*
    "Testify," *West Trestle Review* Pushcart Nominee
    "Young's Literal Translation," *Virginia's Best Emerging Poets*

About the Author

LATORIAL FAISON is an American poet, author, veteran military spouse, mother, and Assistant Professor of English. Her writing continues the African American literary tradition and explores the intersections of the Black experience in terms of race, place, culture, and identity. Faison's poetry and creative nonfiction have been published in *Callaloo, Obsidian: Literature and Art in the African Diaspora, Aunt Chloe, Stonecoast Review, Artemis Journal, Prairie Schooner, West Trestle Review, The Southern Poetry Anthology, Southern Women's Review, About Place Journal, Deep South Magazine, Taj Mahal Review, Untenured,* and others. She is the author of *The Missed Education of the Negro: An Examination of the Black Segregated Experience in Southampton County, Virginia 1950–1970;* poetry collections *Mother to Son, I Am Woman, Love Poems, Immaculate Perceptions, Secrets of My Soul;* the trilogy collection *28 Days of Poetry Celebrating Black History;* and children's books *Kendall's Golf Lesson* and *100 Poems You Can Write: A Poetry Journal for Kids of All Ages*. A Tom Howard Poetry Prize recipient and Pushcart nominee, Faison has also been awarded fellowships from Furious Flower Poetry Center, Virginia Humanities, and the Association of Writers & Writing Programs. She currently serves on the faculty of Virginia State University. Faison is married to her high school sweetheart, a retired US Army Colonel; they have three sons.

www.ingramcontent.com/pod-product-compliance
Lightning Source LLC
Chambersburg PA
CBHW061751070526
44585CB00025B/2859